Diplodocus
dih-PLOD-uh-kus

Triceratops
try-SERRA-tops

Tyrannosaurus
tie-RAN-o-saw-rus

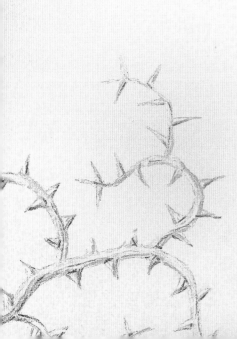

Kronosaurus
kro-no-saw-rus

To Joe Luis Young

from Old Tony Mitton

—T.M.

For Fynnjan and

dinosaur lovers everywhere!

—L.C.

Text copyright © 2009 by Tony Mitton
Illustrations copyright © 2009 by Lynne Chapman
KINGFISHER
Published in the United States by Kingfisher, an imprint of Henry Holt
and Company LLC, 175 Fifth Avenue, New York, New York 10010.
First published in Great Britain by Kingfisher Publications plc,
an imprint of Macmillan Children's Books, London.
All rights reserved

Distributed in Canada by H. B. Fenn and Company Ltd.

Library of Congress Cataloging-in-Publication Data
has been applied for.

ISBN: 978-0-7534-6226-3

Kingfisher books are available for special promotions and premiums.
For details contact: Director of Special Markets, Holtzbrinck Publishers.

First American Edition September 2009
Printed in China
10 9 8 7 6 5 4 3 2 1
1TR/0309/LFG/UNTD/157MA/C

Gnash, Gnaw, DINOSAUR!

Prehistoric poems with lift-the-flap surprises!

Written by
Tony Mitton

Illustrated by
Lynne Chapman

KINGFISHER
NEW YORK

We lived long ago . . .

We're back in this book with a big hello.
Come and see us moving as we slosh through the swamp.
Come and watch us eating as we chomp, chomp, chomp.
Some of us are massive and tower up tall.
Some of us are tiny, ever so small.
Some roam the prairie, some swim the sea,
and some ride the breezes, flying 'round free.
There are many kinds of dinosaur here for you to meet.
So dip into these pages for a dinosaur treat . . .

Diplodocus

Diplodocus. That's me. Hello.

With my long, lithe neck, I can sweep around low.

If I see lush leaves at the top of the trees,

I can crane up high and crop them with ease.

But although I am peaceful and plodding and slow,

if you annoy me, you'll get a hard blow.

Don't try to fight me, to bite and to rip,

or you'll learn that my tail is a strong, swift whip!

Pteranodon

I am Pteranodon. Just look at meeeeeeeee!
Sweeping and gliding and flying so freeeeeeeee!

Ace hang glider, air-current rider, cliff-top swooper, cool loop-the-looper -
Watch how my leathery wings spread wide,
helping me hover and wheel and glide.
Watch how I whirl from the cliffs with a wheeeeeeeee!
swooping to scoop up a fish from the sea.

Tyrannosaurus

I'm Tyrannosaurus. I am the boss.
I'm also the fiercest. So don't make me cross.

My legs are like pillars. They shudder the ground.
The others all tremble to hear such a sound.
They try to avoid me. They fear for their necks . . .

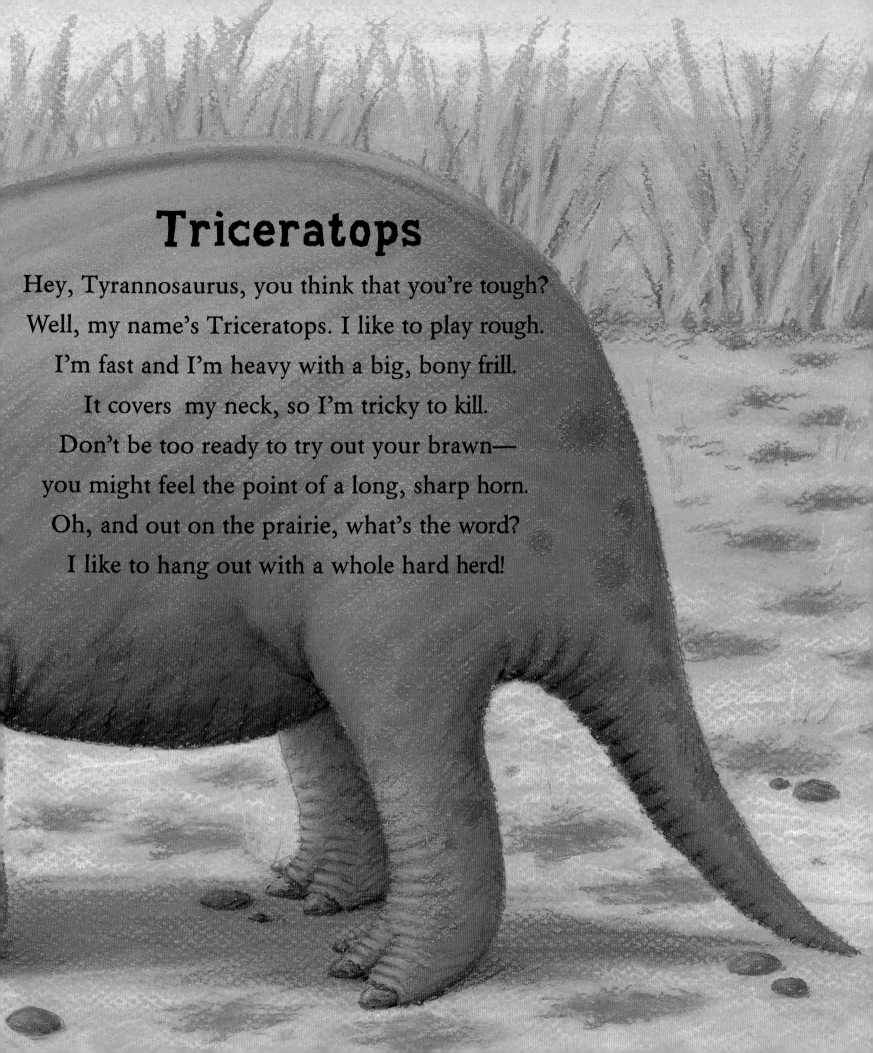

Triceratops

Hey, Tyrannosaurus, you think that you're tough?

Well, my name's Triceratops. I like to play rough.

I'm fast and I'm heavy with a big, bony frill.

It covers my neck, so I'm tricky to kill.

Don't be too ready to try out your brawn—

you might feel the point of a long, sharp horn.

Oh, and out on the prairie, what's the word?

I like to hang out with a whole hard herd!

Kronosaurus

I am big-head Kronosaurus, monster of the deep.
Gliding through the ocean, I doze but never sleep.
Fear me in the daylight, fear me in the dark,
fear me for I seem to be a prehistoric shark.
My jaws are really massive. My paddles give me speed . . .

Mononykus

Look at me, Mononykus. What on earth am I?

A weird kind of dino bird that cannot even fly.

My wings look like a ballet skirt, a funny mass of fluff.

They make me seem so silly—I wish that I looked tough.

I'd like to be a dinosaur but have to be a bird,

and with my beak and feathers—well, don't I look absurd?

Deinonychus

We are the deinonychuses, ready to attack.
Watch us as we race along, running in a pack.

We're cunning, yes, we're clever, and we mean to get our prey.
We hunt it down together, so it never gets away.

Our toenails are our weapons. Each one is like a knife.
So when you hear us coming,

Pteranodon

was more like a glider than a bird!
It had a wingspan of 23 feet.

Deinonychus

was about the same size as
an adult human being.

Mononykus

had stumpy wings that were
not used for flying. It might have
used them for balance.